A Look at
GLACIERS

Patrick Allen

The Rosen Publishing Group's
PowerKids Press™
New York

Published in 2009 by The Rosen Publishing Group, Inc.
29 East 21st Street, New York, NY 10010

Book Design: Dan Hosek and Michael J. Flynn

Photo Credits: Cover © Cornel Achirei/Shutterstock; p. 4 © Paul Souders/Corbis; p. 5 © Peter Zaharov/Shutterstock; p. 7 (glacier) © Svetlana Privezentseva/Shutterstock; p. 7 (inset) http://upload.wikimedia.org/wikipedia/commons/a/ac/Firn_from_South_Cascade_Glacier.jpg; pp. 8, 25 © Arctic-Images/Corbis; p. 9 © Jakub Cejpek/Shutterstock; p. 10 (glacier) © Peter Wey/Shutterstock; p. 10 (inset) http://upload.wikimedia.org/wikipedia/commons/9/93/ByrdGlacier_HiLoContrast.jpg; p. 11 © Ashley Cooper/Corbis; p. 12 © Bryan Busovicki/Shutterstock; p. 13 © Peter Johnson/Corbis; p. 14 (iceberg) © Susannah Grant/Shutterstock; p. 14 (valley glacier) © Christopher Walker/Shutterstock; p. 15 (calving glacier) © Vera Bogaerts/Shutterstock; p. 17 © Jozef Sedmak/Shutterstock; p. 18 © Rafael Martin-Gaitero/Shutterstock; p. 20 © Martine Oger/Shutterstock; p. 21 © SF photo/Shutterstock; p. 23 (Grinnell Glacier 1981) http://upload.wikimedia.org/wikipedia/commons/9/96/Grinnell_Glacier_1981.jpg; p. 23 (Grinnell Glacier 2005) http://upload.wikimedia.org/wikipedia/commons/5/51/Grinnell_Glacier_2005.jpg; p. 24 © Morton Beebe/Corbis; p. 26 © Vienna Report Agency/Sygma/Corbis; p. 27 © Claus Felix/epa/Corbis; p. 28 © Keith Levit/Shutterstock; p. 29 © kkaplin/Shutterstock.

Library of Congress Cataloging-in-Publication Data

Allen, Patrick D.
  A look at glaciers / Patrick Allen.
      p. cm. — (Real life readers)
  Includes index.
  ISBN: 978-1-4358-0147-9
  6-pack ISBN: 978-1-4358-0148-6
  ISBN 978-1-4358-2982-4 (library binding)
  1. Glaciers—Juvenile literature. I. Title.
  GB2403.8.A45 2009
  551.31'2—dc22

                                        2008036801

Manufactured in the United States of America

Contents

What Is a Glacier?

A glacier is a large mass of ice that moves slowly over land. It's actually a river of ice! Glaciers exist in every part of the world. They can be found in places that are cold year-round, such as the North and South Poles and mountainous regions. A glacier's size may change over time depending on how much **precipitation** falls and how much melting occurs.

In recent years, world **temperatures** have been rising, which has caused glaciers to melt more than usual. Should people worry about what will happen to glaciers? In this book, we'll take a look at how glaciers form, how they've shaped the land, and how their future will affect the entire world.

melting glacier

Scientists study glaciers, such as this one atop
Mount Kilimanjaro in Africa, and how they move.

In many parts of the world, snow melts completely as winter turns to spring, so glaciers can't form. Glaciers can only grow in places that are very cold all year. In these areas, layers of snow pile up over time. As each layer pushes down on the layers below it, the weight causes the snowflakes to form small, hard ice **pellets** called **firn**. Scientists think it takes about 1 year for firn to form.

New layers of snow on top of the firn push out air and bond the ice pellets. When the layers of snow become 50 feet (15 m) or more deep, the weight presses the firn into **dense** crystals of glacial ice. As long as more snow falls than **evaporates**, the glacier continues to grow.

How a Glacier Forms

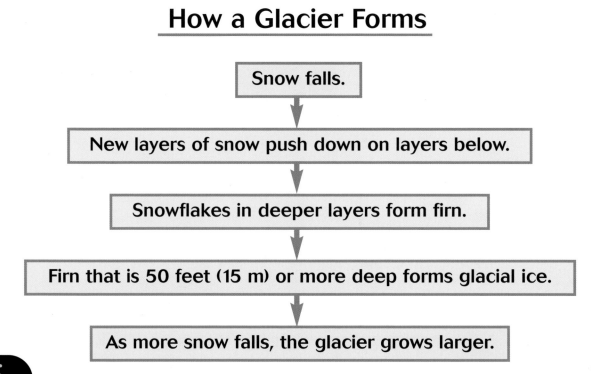

Snow falls.

New layers of snow push down on layers below.

Snowflakes in deeper layers form firn.

Firn that is 50 feet (15 m) or more deep forms glacial ice.

As more snow falls, the glacier grows larger.

firn up close

Most glaciers are about 300 to 10,000 feet (90 to 3,000 m) thick.
Thick glaciers may look blue.

The Glacier Moves

Gravity is the force that pulls everything toward Earth. It gives things weight. It also moves glaciers. Ice crystals within a glacier can shift when weight presses down on them. Even a small change can affect the whole glacier—like a ripple in a pond. Movement within the glacier may cause its mass to spread out.

Glacial ice moving even the smallest distance over Earth's surface causes **friction**. Friction creates heat, which melts the glacier's bottom layer. Warmth from within Earth may also melt the glacier's bottom layer. In addition, water may seep to the bottom through **crevasses** in the glacier. Water beneath the glacier helps it move more easily and more quickly.

You can see where layers of ice have collapsed or shifted in some glaciers, such as the ones shown above and at left.

buried
crevasses —

flow lines —

Byrd
Glacier

This picture shows a glacier with narrow cracks, or crevasses, visible on its surface. The inset shows a glacier that flows much like a river. You can also see that crevasses can be hidden beneath a smooth surface.

The movement of a glacier depends upon the amount of water beneath it, the angle of the slope, and the surface beneath the glacier. Most glaciers move less than 1 foot (30 cm) per day. Sometimes a glacier may move more than 100 feet (30 m) per day. Scientists can find the speed of a glacier's movement by putting stakes in the ice and measuring how much they move over a period of time. They also use cameras and dyes.

The bottom and sides of a glacier move more slowly than the rest because of friction against the ground. Parts moving at different speeds cause the glacier's shape to change. The more the glacier moves, the more changes occur. Movement over uneven land or changes in speed can cause crevasses as well.

Ice Sheets

Ice-sheet glaciers are found on level land. Continental glaciers are thick ice sheets that cover very large areas. They cover all but the highest mountain peaks of Antarctica and Greenland. If these glaciers were to melt, sea levels around the world would rise hundreds of feet!

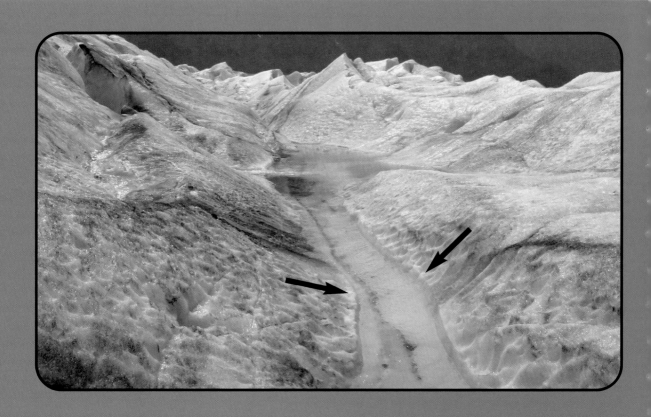

This photo shows an Alaskan outlet glacier, a fast-moving stream of ice flowing through a more slowly moving ice sheet.

ice shelf

Ice shelves are created by gravity spreading ice-sheet glaciers out over the water. Only Antarctica, Greenland, and Canada have ice shelves.

Other kinds of ice sheets include ice caps, which are shaped like **domes** and are smaller than continental glaciers. They cover less than 19,500 square miles (50,500 sq km). Ice fields are about the same size as ice caps, but they're flat.

Valley Glaciers

When glaciers form on mountains, they move down into valleys and form long, narrow bodies of ice called valley glaciers. There are several kinds of valley glaciers.

Valley glaciers that reach the sea are called tidewater glaciers. Icebergs may break off tidewater glaciers. This is called calving. The largest tidewater glacier in North America is the Hubbard Glacier, located in Alaska and the Yukon Territory of Canada. Icebergs as tall as buildings break off this glacier.

tidewater glacier

iceberg

Valley glaciers that flow into flat plains are called piedmont glaciers. These widen into a bulblike shape as they flow. Hanging glaciers are valley glaciers that end at or near the top of a cliff. These may cause **avalanches**.

calving glacier

The picture above shows Alaska's Meares Glacier calving.
The icebergs that break off will be larger than they look.
Ninety percent of an iceberg is underwater.

How a Moving Glacier Changes the Land

Glacier movement **erodes** the land beneath. When a glacier surges, or moves forward, it picks up rocks. The rocks may become a part of the glacier as ice refreezes around them. The rocks scrape the surface beneath the glacier, like sandpaper. When a glacier retreats, or shrinks, it leaves behind till—clay, small rocks, sand, and dirt. Till makes excellent farmland.

New landforms result when glaciers surge and retreat. Till can form long, narrow hills called moraines (muh-RAYNZ). Fjords (fee-OHRDZ) are long coastal valleys carved by glaciers and flooded with ocean water. Glaciers also create cirques (SURKS), which are bowl-shaped hollows in mountainsides. When two cirques meet, they create a sharp crest in the mountainside called an arête (uh-RAYT).

Cirques and arêtes in the European Alps created the famous horn shape of the Matterhorn mountain.

▶

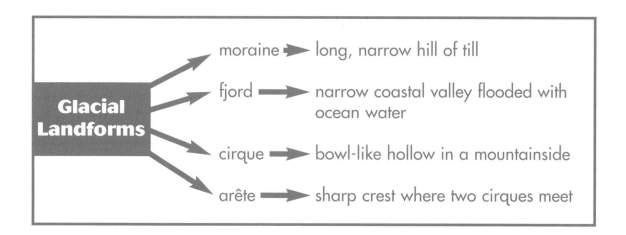

Glacial Landforms

moraine ➡	long, narrow hill of till
fjord ➡	narrow coastal valley flooded with ocean water
cirque ➡	bowl-like hollow in a mountainside
arête ➡	sharp crest where two cirques meet

Ice Ages

Ice sheets once covered much of Earth during periods of time called ice ages. An ice age lasts about 100,000 years. As many as eighteen ice ages made up the last glacial **epoch**, which scientists call the Pleistocene (PLYS-tuh-seen).

About 55 million years ago, Earth's atmosphere began cooling off. About 38 million years ago, glaciers began forming in Antarctica. Over 25 million years, they grew to be an ice sheet. About 7 million years ago, ice sheets began forming over North America, Europe, and Asia. The last ice age ended about 11,500 years ago.

Some scientists think glacial epochs happen in cycles. They think Earth's atmosphere will eventually cool again, allowing more glaciers to form around the world once again.

◀ When another glacial epoch occurs, much of Earth will be covered by glaciers like this one in Argentina.

Some Pleistocene glaciers grew to be about 10,000 feet (3,000 m) thick. As the glaciers grew, they drew in so much water that sea levels all over the world dropped, uncovering land.

Around 36,000 years ago, a land bridge connecting northeastern Asia to northwestern North America appeared. This land bridge allowed people to travel to and settle in North America for the first time. When the ice age ended, water from melting glaciers covered the land bridge. Today, a narrow body of water called the Bering Strait runs through this area, separating Russia and Alaska.

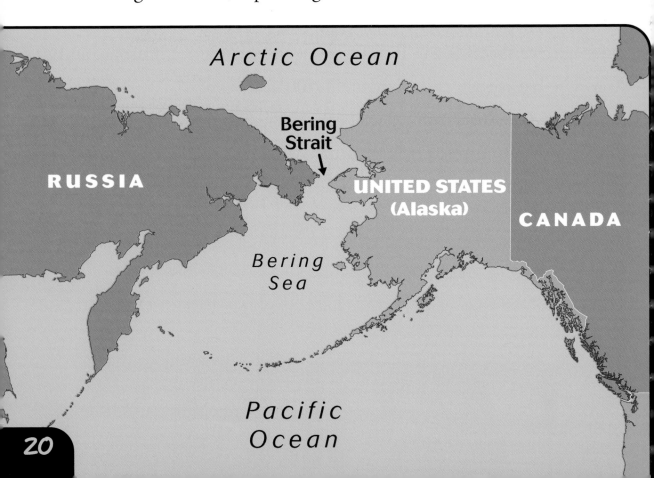

Niagara River

Canada

United States

Niagara Falls

In North America, glaciers formed the Great Lakes. Scientists think the last ice sheet around Lake Erie melted about 12,000 years ago. The lake overflowed and formed the Niagara River, which then formed Niagara Falls. An entire section of New York State—Long Island—was formed by till left by glaciers!

Scientists think the land bridge connected Asia and North America for about 18,000 years!

Glacier National Park

Glacier National Park is located in Montana on the border between the United States and Canada. Over fifty mountain glaciers of various sizes can be found in the park's Rocky Mountains. These glaciers are considered "new" since they formed in the last few thousand years. The largest glacier, Grinnell Glacier, is about 1.5 miles (2.4 km) long and about 1 mile (1.6 km) wide. It's 500 feet (152 m) thick at some parts.

The park also has about 250 lakes. Even in summer, icebergs float in Iceberg Lake, which is located in a cirque.

Because Glacier National Park contains so many glaciers and glacial landforms, it's a center for glacier study. Scientists have been closely watching the rate of glacial melting in the park over recent years.

Canada

Glacier National Park

United States

**Grinnell Glacier
1981**

These pictures show how
Grinnell Glacier in
Glacier National Park
has melted over the years due
to warmer temperatures.

**Grinnell Glacier
2005**

Glaciers: Keys to the Past

Since glaciers are thousands or millions of years old, they tell us about Earth's past. Scientists can drill deep into glaciers and take out samples called ice cores. Methods of dating ice cores vary. Sometimes layers of ice can be counted and each may represent 1 year. The deeper the core sample, the more the firn is packed together. It's harder to identify how old a deeper sample is, but scientists have found ways.

This scientist is drilling an ice core. Since the deeper parts of glaciers were formed longer ago, scientists can learn more about Earth's distant past by drilling deeper ice cores.

ice core sample

Within the ice cores are bubbles of trapped air. The air can be tested to find out what Earth's climate was like at different times and what gases were in the atmosphere. This can help us understand the conditions that cause an ice age and guess when another may occur. Ice cores can even tell us about plants and animals that lived on Earth long ago.

The "Iceman"

In 1991, two Germans made a discovery while hiking in the Alps between Austria and Italy. Helmut and Erika Simon found a body sticking out of a glacier. The glacier was melting, revealing most of the body. Scientists determined the **mummy** was from about 3300 B.C.!

The body had frozen soon after the man died, so the mummy was well preserved. The man was about 30 years old when he died. He was wearing leather clothes and shoes. From matter found on his teeth, scientists found out what he had eaten before he died. They could even tell where he grew up and where he later lived! The mummy was named Oetzi for the area where he was found. Today, Oetzi is displayed in a museum in Italy.

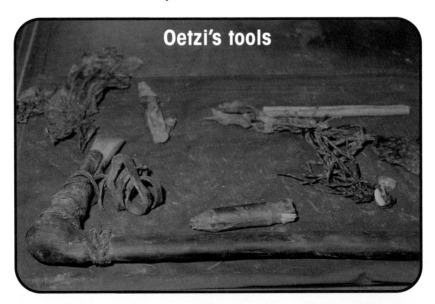

Oetzi's tools

In this photo, Erika and Helmut Simon hold up a book with a picture of the body they found. Oetzi died from a wound in his shoulder. He may have been a warrior.

Global Warming and Glaciers

Global warming is an increase in the average temperature of Earth's atmosphere. The average temperature has risen about 1°F (0.6°C) over the last century. This small change has greatly affected the world's glaciers. Some scientists think the glaciers in the Alps could melt completely by 2050. Glaciers in other parts of the world—even Antarctica and Greenland—are disappearing, too. Scientists are worried that people's use of coal, electricity, and oil is making global warming worse.

Scientists think global warming will cause polar bears, which live on glaciers around the North Pole, to die out. Penguins at the South Pole (shown on page 29) need their icy surroundings to survive as well.

As glaciers disappear, they can create problems. Glaciers hold almost 70 percent of the world's freshwater. If they melt, much of their freshwater would flow into the oceans' salt water. That would affect ocean animals and plants. Also, sea levels around the world would rise, flooding coastal areas. This would harm plants, animals, and people in many ways.

The consequences of losing glaciers around the world are far-reaching. We must learn how we can protect glaciers and slow the disappearance of some of nature's most amazing creations.

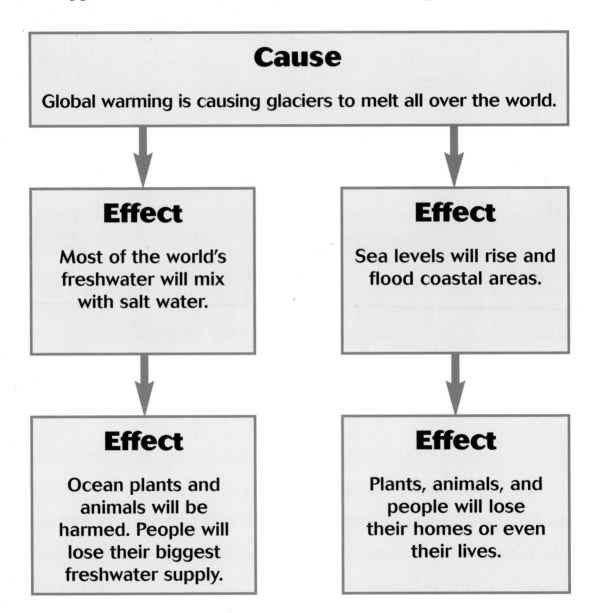

Cause

Global warming is causing glaciers to melt all over the world.

Effect

Most of the world's freshwater will mix with salt water.

Effect

Sea levels will rise and flood coastal areas.

Effect

Ocean plants and animals will be harmed. People will lose their biggest freshwater supply.

Effect

Plants, animals, and people will lose their homes or even their lives.

Glossary

avalanche (AA-vuh-lanch) A large amount of snow, ice, earth, or rock rushing suddenly down a mountainside.

crevasse (krih-VAHS) A deep, narrow opening in a glacier.

dense (DEHNS) Tightly packed together.

dome (DOHM) A semicircular shape that slopes down.

epoch (EH-pahk) A long period of time in Earth's geologic history.

erode (ih-ROHD) To wear away over time.

evaporate (ih-VA-puh-rayt) To change from a liquid to a gas.

firn (FIHRN) Small, hard pellets of snow in upper layers of a glacier.

friction (FRIHK-shun) The force that resists motion between two things rubbing against each other.

mummy (MUH-mee) A dead body that has been kept from rotting.

pellet (PEH-luht) A small, dense body of matter.

precipitation (prih-sih-puh-TAY-shun) Any moisture that falls from the sky. Rain and snow are precipitation.

temperature (TEHM-puhr-chur) How hot or cold something is.

Index